Becoming a Project Management King or Queen (Life® After the PMP Exam)

Life After the PMP® Exam

PHILL AKINWALE, OPM3, PMP, PMI-ACP

Praizi⬤nMed a
Real World Project Management Training Solutions

Becoming a Project Management King or Queen (Life After the PMP® Exam)
Published by Praizion Media
P.O Box 22241, Mesa, AZ 85277
E-mail: info@praizion.com
www.praizion.com
Author
Phillip Akinwale, MSc, OPM3, PMP, PMI-ACP, CAPM, PSM, CSM

ISBN 978-1-934579-32-9

9 781934 579329

CONTENTS

Introduction

Every year, countless students achieve the esteemed PMP certification, marking a significant milestone in their professional journey. Yet, this accomplishment is but the dawn of the odyssey for a certified project manager. While some soar to unparalleled heights, others find themselves anchored to their initial position, and a few even grapple with a growing disillusionment, having anticipated a world brimming with opportunities.

However, it is essential to understand that success, much like charity, does not always present itself without effort or initiative. At times, opportunities must be ardently pursued before they manifest. On other occasions, they elude even the certified, not because of the absence of knowledge, but due to a lack of preparation to seize them. This shortfall might stem from an inability to demonstrate expertise, a lack of confidence, or perhaps an inadequacy in articulating one's capabilities compellingly.

In my years of mentoring and coaching project managers, I've encountered many who grapple with these challenges.

Some battle the crippling weight of imposter syndrome, while others are so engrossed in their niche that they remain oblivious to the vast expanse of opportunities around them. Some even misunderstand the essence of leadership. These observations became the foundation for this book: a guide to navigating life after the PMP exam and truly harnessing the power of your certification.

Whether you're contending with a lackadaisical approach, the shadows of imposter syndrome, or a narrow perspective that blinds you to broader horizons, this book is your compass. It's a testament to my belief that every project manager can ascend to their unique pinnacle of success.

Your "next level" might differ from your peers, but it's a summit worth striving for. I hope this book illuminates your path, encouraging you to embrace continuous learning, seek clarity in your quest, and foster an unwavering positive mindset. As you turn the page, may you be inspired to not just dream, but to actualize your aspirations.

Chapter 1: The Road to Success

"Success is... knowing your purpose in life, growing to reach your maximum potential, and sowing seeds that benefit others." – John C. Maxwell

Success, a term often uttered but seldom understood in its entirety, is a mosaic of perceptions, aspirations, and accomplishments. At its core, success is not merely a destination or a trophy to be showcased. It's an intricate tapestry woven with threads of contentment, achievement, significance, and purpose. While its definition may vary from one soul to another, the path leading to it often treads common ground.

Success isn't merely an endgame; it's a state of being, a mindset that resonates with contentment, achievement, and significance. It's an ever-evolving dance between our perceptions, societal expectations, and the myriad variables that shape our journey. If you let the world dictate your success, its authenticity becomes questionable. However, when you craft your own definition, you wield the power to steer your journey with purpose.

At the heart of success lies genuine human connection. It's about fostering relationships built on sincerity and genuine care. In a world often masked by facades, genuine relationships built on sincerity and care stand out as beacons of hope. Authenticity, in its raw and unfiltered form, becomes the compass guiding us towards genuine success.

Authenticity, in all its forms, is the compass that points towards true success. Furthermore, success thrives on the principle of reciprocity. The more value you infuse into the world, the more enriched your own journey becomes. As a mentor and coach, I've discovered that imparting knowledge not only benefits the learner but also deepens my own understanding. Knowledge, when shared, multiplies in value and keeps the flame of learning alive.

Your mindset, too, plays a pivotal role. Your mindset, that internal compass, plays an instrumental role in shaping your journey. A mindset shrouded in negativity can ensnare you, hindering progress. On the other hand, a mindset radiating positivity becomes the wind propelling you forward, allowing you to soar to new heights.

A negative mindset can be a quagmire, pulling you into a vortex of stagnation. In contrast, a positive mindset is the wind beneath your wings. As the wise Zig Ziglar once said, "It's your attitude, not your aptitude, that determines your altitude." Success, then, is as much about perspective as it is about skill.

Leadership, in its truest form, is the cornerstone of success.

It's about embodying excellence, championing value, and making informed decisions. A true leader is a beacon of influence, leading not from a pedestal but from the trenches, exemplifying servant leadership, collaboration, and emotional intelligence.

Success is not a destination but a journey, a continuous quest for growth and evolution. It demands a clear vision, a guiding light that illuminates your path. Whether your vision is to revolutionize industries or to master your craft, it's the missions, objectives, and key results that pave the way. As life unfolds, it's essential to remain agile, adapting and refining your vision to stay relevant in an ever-changing world.

Success is an ever-evolving narrative, shaped by our perceptions, societal benchmarks, and the countless variables that punctuate our journey. Entrusting the world to define your success can lead to a mirage, an illusion that might shimmer from afar but lacks substance. However, when you sculpt your own definition, you become the master of your destiny, navigating with intention and clarity.

Success beyond your certification or current state is a journey, an odyssey of self-discovery, growth, and evolution. It beckons for a vision, a lighthouse guiding you through the tumultuous seas of life. Whether your vision is grandiose or intimately personal, it's the missions, objectives, and key results that carve the path forward.

Life, in its unpredictable splendor, necessitates agility. As the sands shift beneath our feet, refining and recalibrating our vision ensures we remain anchored in relevance.

In conclusion, I echo the wisdom of John Maxwell, encapsulated in what I coined as "The KGS principle": Knowing your purpose, Growing to your fullest potential, and Sowing seeds for the greater good. This, dear reader, is the essence of true success. Embrace it, live it, and let it guide you to unparalleled heights.

Chapter 2: Introduction to Project Leadership

"The function of leadership is to produce more leaders, not more followers." - Ralph Nader.

This chapter introduces you to the essence of project management leadership. It's about more than ticking off tasks on a checklist; it's about fostering a spirit of drive and ambition that propels the entire team towards success.

Project Management Leadership plays a crucial role in organizations, facilitating the successful execution of projects and contributing to overall business success. Project managers are responsible for planning, organizing, and managing projects to achieve specific objectives within defined constraints like scope, time, and budget. Their role extends beyond task management, as they must also possess the ability to inspire, motivate, and lead their teams to achieve project goals effectively.

1.1 The Difference Between Project Managers and Project Leaders:

While project managers focus on executing tasks and adhering to established processes, project leaders go beyond these responsibilities. They are visionaries who inspire others to work together towards a common goal. Project leaders drive progress and innovation by encouraging creativity, embracing change, and fostering a culture of continuous improvement. Unlike mere task managers, project leaders take ownership of the project's success and are willing to take calculated risks to achieve exceptional results.

1.2 The Servant vs. Leader Dichotomy:

1.2.1 Servant Leadership in Project Management: Servant leadership is a leadership philosophy that centers around the idea of serving others first, prioritizing the needs of team members, and enabling their personal and professional growth. In the context of project management, a servant leader seeks to understand the strengths and weaknesses of their team members and provides the necessary support, resources, and guidance to help them succeed. This approach fosters a collaborative and inclusive environment, where every team member's voice is valued, and decision-making is participative.

1.2.2 Benefits of Servant Leadership in Project Management:

- Improved Team Morale: Servant leaders create a positive and empowering work environment, leading to higher team morale and job satisfaction.

- Enhanced Team Performance: By nurturing the development of team members, servant leaders unlock their full potential, resulting in improved overall team performance.

- Increased Accountability: Team members are more likely to take ownership of their responsibilities when they feel supported and valued by their leader.

- Adaptability and Flexibility: Servant leaders encourage open communication and feedback, making it easier to adapt to changes and overcome challenges.

1.2.3 Potential Downsides of Servant Leadership in Project Management:

- Time-Intensive: The servant leadership approach may require more time and effort, as leaders invest in building strong relationships with team members.

- Decision-Making Challenges: In some situations, seeking consensus among team members might slow down decision-making processes, especially when time is of the essence.

1.3 Directive Leadership Style in Project Management:

In contrast to servant leadership, a directive leadership style involves a more top-down, authoritative approach. Project managers employing this style tend to make decisions independently and provide clear instructions to team members regarding what needs to be done. While this approach can be effective in certain contexts, it may not be suitable for all projects.

1.3.1 Contexts for Directive Leadership in Project Management:

- High-Risk Projects: In projects where there is little room for error, a directive leadership style may be necessary to ensure precision and minimize potential risks.

- Fast-Paced Projects: When time is of the essence, quick decision-making is crucial, making a more directive approach preferable.

- Inexperienced Team Members: In situations where team members lack experience or expertise, a directive leader can provide much-needed guidance and clarity.

1.3.2 Drawbacks of Directive Leadership in Project Management:

- Reduced Team Engagement: A highly directive approach may lead to reduced team engagement and creativity, as team members may feel they have little input or autonomy.

- Limited Adaptability: Directive leadership might struggle to adapt to dynamic project environments, where flexibility and creativity are essential.

THE ROLE OF DRIVE IN PROJECT MANAGEMENT

1.4 Ambition, Drive, and Determination in Successful Project Management:

Drive is a critical factor that distinguishes successful project managers from the rest. Ambitious project managers possess the determination and tenacity to overcome obstacles and keep the team focused on achieving project objectives. Their unyielding commitment to success motivates the team to push beyond their limits and deliver exceptional results.

1.4.1 Drive as a Motivational Tool:

A project manager's drive can be infectious, inspiring team members to take ownership of their work and go the extra mile to meet project deadlines and quality standards. It creates a sense of purpose and pride among team members, fostering a high-performance culture.

1.4.2 Drive in the Face of Challenges: Projects often encounter unforeseen challenges and setbacks. A determined project manager does not shy away from such difficulties but tackles them head-on, finding innovative solutions and maintaining team morale throughout the process.

1.4.3 Drive vs. Burnout: While drive is essential, it must be balanced to avoid burnout. Project managers should recognize the signs of overexertion in themselves and their team members, promoting a healthy work-life balance to sustain long-term success.

Conclusion:

Project Management Leadership is a multifaceted role that requires more than just task management. Effective project leaders drive progress and innovation by inspiring their teams, embracing servant leadership principles, and leveraging their ambition and determination to overcome challenges. Understanding the dynamics of leadership styles and the significance of drive in project management can lead to the successful execution of projects and the achievement of organizational objectives.

Chapter 3: The Importance of Continuous Learning

"Learning is not attained by chance, it must be sought for with ardor and attended to with diligence." - Abigail Adams.

This chapter underscores the importance of continuous learning and professional development in the dynamic field of project management. Let's get straight into the main points!

2.1 Avoiding Complacency after Earning a Project Management Certification:

Achieving a project management certification is a significant accomplishment and a testament to one's knowledge and skills in the field. However, the danger lies in complacency, where project managers may become content with their current level of expertise and stop seeking further growth. Complacency can lead to stagnation and hinder a project manager's ability to adapt to new challenges and emerging trends in the industry. It is essential to recognize that project management is a continuously evolving discipline, and what works today may not be sufficient in the future.

2.2 The Importance of Continuous Learning and Skill Development:

Continuous learning and skill development are crucial for project managers to remain effective and successful in their roles. By embracing a mindset of continuous improvement, project managers can:

a. Stay Relevant: The business landscape is ever-changing, with new technologies, methodologies, and best practices emerging regularly. Continuous learning ensures project managers stay relevant and can apply the latest tools and techniques to their projects.

b. Adapt to Challenges: Projects often encounter unexpected challenges, and a project manager's ability to adapt is paramount.

Continuous learning equips them with the necessary knowledge and problem-solving skills to address new obstacles effectively.

c. Enhance Leadership Abilities: Leadership is an integral part of project management. Through ongoing learning, project managers can hone their leadership abilities, communication skills, and emotional intelligence to inspire and lead their teams more effectively.

d. Improve Project Outcomes: Continuous learning leads to improved decision-making and a deeper understanding of project complexities, ultimately resulting in better project outcomes and customer satisfaction.

2.3 The Rapidly Changing Nature of Project Management:

Project management is subject to rapid changes due to technological advancements, market trends, and evolving business practices. New project management methodologies and frameworks are continuously emerging, making it essential for project managers to stay up-to-date to remain effective in their roles.

2.4 The Importance of Understanding the Latest PMBOK® Guide:

The Project Management Body of Knowledge (PMBOK®) Guide, published by the Project Management Institute (PMI), is a globally recognized standard for project management practices. The guide undergoes updates periodically to reflect changes in the industry and lessons learned from successful projects. Understanding the latest PMBOK Guide is critical for project managers, as it provides a comprehensive overview of project management principles and best practices, serving as a valuable reference for their work.

2.5 Learning Opportunities for Continued Development:

To embrace continuous learning and development, project managers can take advantage of various resources, including:

a. Professional Development Workshops and Seminars: Attending workshops and seminars allows project managers to learn from industry experts, exchange ideas with peers, and gain practical insights into new methodologies and tools.

b. Online Courses and Certifications: Online platforms offer a wide range of project management courses and certifications, enabling project managers to study at their own pace and specialize in specific areas of interest.

c. Webinars and Conferences: Participating in webinars and conferences allows project managers to stay updated on the latest trends, research findings, and real-world case studies in project management.

d. Networking and Community Involvement: Engaging with project management communities and professional networks fosters learning through shared experiences and knowledge exchange.

2.6 The Importance of Lifelong Learning in Project Management:

Lifelong learning is a mindset that extends beyond professional development courses and certifications. It involves a commitment to continuous self-improvement and a willingness to seek knowledge and new perspectives throughout one's career. In the dynamic field of project management, embracing lifelong learning enables project managers to remain agile, innovative, and well-equipped to lead successful projects in any context.

Conclusion:

Continuous learning and development are indispensable for project managers aiming to excel in their roles. Avoiding complacency, understanding the rapidly changing nature of project management, and staying updated with the latest PMBOK Guide are essential aspects of this journey. By actively seeking learning opportunities and adopting a mindset of lifelong learning, project managers can enhance their abilities, adapt to challenges, and deliver successful projects that drive organizational success.

Chapter 4: The Power of Conviction and Influence

"People may hear your words, but they feel your attitude." -

John C. Maxwell.

This chapter goes into the power of conviction and the essentiality of influence in successful project management, reminding us that true leadership stems from within.

3.1 The Importance of Conviction:

Conviction refers to the strong beliefs and principles that project managers hold about their work, team, and project goals. Having conviction is crucial for project managers as it provides a sense of purpose and direction, guiding their decision-making and actions throughout the project lifecycle.

a. Guiding Decision-Making: Conviction helps project managers make informed and principled decisions, especially when faced with difficult choices. It ensures that decisions align with the project's vision and goals, contributing to its overall success.

b. Inspiring Team Members: Project managers with conviction inspire and motivate their team members to work with dedication and commitment. When team members witness their leader's passion and belief in the project, they are more likely to share the same enthusiasm and strive for excellence.

c. Overcoming Challenges: In challenging situations, conviction acts as a driving force, encouraging project managers to persevere and find innovative solutions. It instills confidence in the team, boosting morale during tough times.

Example: A project manager leading an environmental sustainability project has a strong conviction about the significance of preserving natural resources for future generations. This conviction influences decisions such as choosing eco-friendly suppliers, implementing energy-saving measures, and advocating for sustainable practices within the organization.

3.2 Becoming Influential:

Being influential within an organization is vital for project managers to gain support, secure necessary resources, and foster a collaborative environment. Several strategies can help project managers become more influential:

a. Communication Skills: Effective communication is key to influence. Project managers should articulate their ideas clearly and persuasively, tailoring their messages to resonate with different stakeholders.

b. Relationship Building: Cultivating positive relationships with stakeholders, team members, and executives enhances a project manager's ability to influence decision-making. Building trust and rapport establishes a strong foundation for collaboration.

c. Demonstrating Competence: Competence breeds confidence and influence. Project managers should showcase their expertise and knowledge to gain respect from their peers and team members.

Example: A project manager seeking to implement a new customer relationship management system understands the concerns of various departments. They communicate the potential benefits of the system clearly and build strong relationships with key stakeholders by addressing their specific needs and demonstrating how the system aligns with the organization's strategic goals.

3.3 Positive Mental Attitude:

Maintaining a positive attitude is crucial for project managers, as it directly impacts their own well-being and that of their team. A positive mental attitude enables project managers to navigate challenges, maintain focus, and foster a constructive project environment.

a. Resilience in the Face of Challenges: A positive attitude helps project managers approach challenges as opportunities for growth and learning, rather than insurmountable obstacles.

b. Team Morale and Productivity: A project manager's positivity can have a ripple effect on the team, boosting morale and productivity. A positive leader inspires confidence and encourages creative problem-solving.

c. Managing Stress: Projects can be stressful, but a positive mindset helps project managers manage stress more effectively, promoting a healthier work environment.

Techniques for Cultivating a Positive Mindset:

i. Practicing Gratitude: Reflecting on and appreciating the positive aspects of the project and team can shift focus away from difficulties.

ii. Emphasizing Progress: Celebrating small victories and acknowledging progress, even amidst challenges, reinforces a positive atmosphere.

iii. Encouraging Team Support: Fostering a supportive team culture where team members help and motivate each other creates a positive and collaborative environment.

Example: A project manager facing delays due to unforeseen circumstances maintains a positive attitude when communicating with the team. They focus on finding solutions, encourage team members to share their ideas, and highlight the progress made despite the setbacks.

Conclusion:

Conviction and influence are powerful attributes that can elevate project managers to achieve outstanding results. Possessing strong beliefs and principles guides decision-making and inspires the team. Becoming influential through effective communication, relationship-building, and competence enables project managers to gain support and collaboration within the organization. Maintaining a positive attitude empowers project managers to navigate challenges, boost team morale, and create a conducive environment for project success. By harnessing the power of conviction and influence while cultivating a positive mindset, project managers can lead their teams to achieve remarkable outcomes and drive organizational success.

Chapter 5: The Role of Relationships and Networking

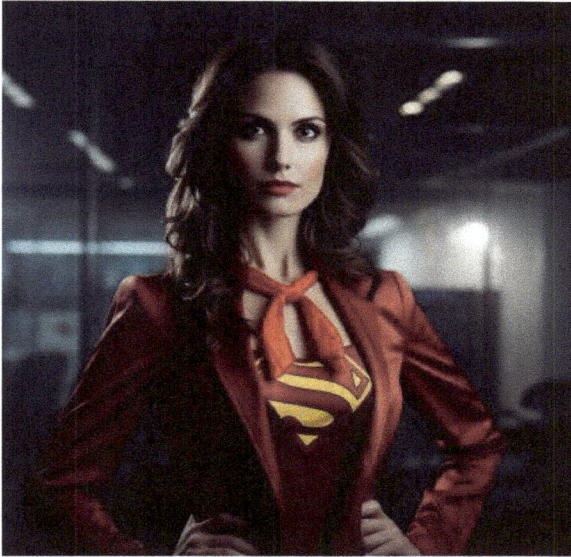

"The currency of real networking is not greed but generosity." - *Keith Ferrazzi.*

In this chapter, we'll explore the invaluable role of relationships and networking in project management, and how they can elevate your career to new heights.

Success isn't just about hitting personal goals or ticking boxes. It's also about understanding and getting along with people. Everyone has their quirks and mistakes, and part of being successful is being patient and understanding with others, especially when we remember we have our own flaws too.

Think about it this way: everyone's doing the best they can with what they've got. Their experiences, their feelings, and even their upbringing play a part in how they act. Some people behave a certain way because it's just how they're wired. This mindset has really helped me get why some people act the way they do.

It's also important to remember we don't have all the answers. Just because we think or work a certain way doesn't mean it's the only way or even the best way. Being open to how others do things can teach us a lot. There's often more than one way to tackle a problem, and by being open-minded, we can achieve more and build better relationships.

In short, a big part of success is about understanding and working well with others. It's about respect, patience, and remembering that everyone's journey is unique. Recognizing the inherent imperfections in each of us is pivotal. Every individual, no matter how accomplished, carries a mosaic of flaws and failures.

True success lies not in mere tolerance but in embracing and assimilating these imperfections, both in ourselves and in others.

It's about extending the hand of patience, seeking to fathom the depths of another's perspective, and grounding ourselves in the belief that everyone is navigating their journey with the tools they possess – be it their emotions, intellect, or experiences.

4.1 Building Relationships:

In project management, building strong relationships with team members, stakeholders, and senior management is fundamental to project success and personal growth as a project manager. These relationships foster trust, open communication, and collaboration, creating a supportive project environment.

a. Importance of Team Relationships: A cohesive and motivated team is essential for project success. Building positive relationships with team members promotes a sense of belonging, encourages teamwork, and enhances overall productivity.

b. Engaging Stakeholders: Stakeholders play a crucial role in project outcomes. Establishing and maintaining positive relationships with stakeholders ensures their active involvement, support, and buy-in throughout the project lifecycle.

c. Influence of Senior Management: Strong relationships with senior management can lead to greater support for the project, access to necessary resources, and increased visibility for the project manager's achievements.

Strategies for Building and Maintaining Relationships:

i. Active Listening: Actively listening to team members and stakeholders demonstrates respect and empathy, fostering stronger connections and understanding.

ii. Regular Communication: Maintaining open and regular communication channels encourages transparency and ensures that everyone remains informed and engaged.

iii. Celebrating Successes: Acknowledging and celebrating individual and team achievements reinforces positive relationships and boosts morale.

iv. Addressing Conflicts: Addressing conflicts promptly and professionally helps prevent issues from escalating and strengthens trust within the team and with stakeholders.

v. Understanding Individual Motivations: Recognizing and understanding what motivates team members and stakeholders enables project managers to tailor their approach and provide appropriate support.

4.2 Networking for Success:

Networking is a powerful tool for career development and professional growth in project management. By establishing connections with peers, industry experts, and potential mentors, project managers can gain valuable insights, opportunities, and support throughout their careers.

a. Broadening Perspectives: Networking exposes project managers to diverse perspectives, best practices, and innovative ideas from other professionals in the field.

b. Access to Opportunities: Through networking, project managers may learn about potential job openings, collaborations, or projects that align with their interests and aspirations.

c. Personal Branding: Effective networking allows project managers to showcase their skills, knowledge, and accomplishments, enhancing their personal brand within the industry.

Tips for Effective Networking:

i. Attend Industry Events: Participating in conferences, workshops, and seminars provides opportunities to meet like-minded professionals and industry leaders.

ii. Utilize Online Platforms: Joining professional networks and forums, such as LinkedIn groups, allows project managers to connect with colleagues globally.

iii. Be Genuine: Authenticity is crucial in networking. Building meaningful connections requires being genuine and showing a sincere interest in others.

iv. Offer Value: Networking is a two-way street. Project managers can offer their expertise or assistance to others, fostering reciprocal relationships.

v. Follow Up: After networking events, follow up with new connections to reinforce the relationship and express gratitude for the interaction.

4.3 Learning from Others:

Learning from others' experiences and perspectives is a valuable aspect of continuous improvement in project management. By seeking feedback and insights from peers, team members, and stakeholders, project managers can enhance their skills and refine their approaches.

a. Gaining New Insights: Learning from others provides project managers with fresh perspectives and ideas, helping them identify blind spots and opportunities for growth.

b. Preventing Mistakes: Embracing feedback and learning from others' experiences can prevent the repetition of common mistakes and improve project outcomes.

c. Strengthening Collaboration: Seeking and incorporating feedback fosters a culture of collaboration and continuous improvement within the project team.

Strategies for Seeking and Incorporating Feedback:

i. Create a Safe Environment: Establish an environment where team members feel comfortable providing honest feedback without fear of repercussions.

ii. Ask Specific Questions: When seeking feedback, ask specific questions related to performance, processes, and project management practices.

iii. Welcome Constructive Criticism: Embrace constructive criticism as an opportunity for growth, rather than a personal attack.

iv. Act on Feedback: Actively incorporating feedback into future decisions and actions demonstrates a commitment to improvement.

v. Foster a Learning Culture: Encourage a culture where learning from others is celebrated and valued, promoting knowledge-sharing among team members.

Conclusion:

Remember the critical role of relationships and networking in project management. Building strong relationships with team members, stakeholders, and senior management fosters trust and collaboration, leading to project success. Networking empowers project managers with valuable insights, opportunities, and personal growth, enhancing their professional journey. Learning from others through feedback and shared experiences promotes continuous improvement and a positive project environment. By embracing the power of relationships, effective networking, and learning from others, project managers can navigate their careers with confidence and drive exceptional project outcomes.

Remember, aspire to constantly believe that people are doing the best with what they have. This perspective, often championed in coaching, has been a beacon in my interactions. It's allowed me to decipher the motivations and actions of those around me, recognizing that behavior often stems from deeply ingrained dispositions and perceptions.

We must remember that our lens to the world isn't the only one. Our convictions, no matter how deeply held, don't hold a monopoly on truth. Just as a prism refracts light in myriad ways, there are countless approaches to a single challenge.

Being open to the kaleidoscope of ideas and methodologies others bring to the table not only enriches our understanding but also fosters collaboration and mutual respect. It's a humbling realization that our way, though effective for us, might not be the sole path to success. By embracing this ethos, we cultivate an environment where diverse perspectives thrive, leading to innovative solutions and deeper connections.

In essence, the pinnacle of success is not just about individual accomplishments. It's about mastering the art of human connection, understanding, and collaboration. For in the dance of human interactions, understanding and empathy are the rhythms that lead to true harmony and success.

Chapter 6: Training, Coaching, and Mentoring

"We are what we repeatedly do. Excellence, then, is not an act,

but a habit." - Aristotle.

This chapter emphasizes the significance of ongoing training, coaching, and mentoring in achieving excellence and mastering the art of project management.

5.1 Continuing Education:

In the dynamic field of project management, ongoing training and education are essential for project managers to stay relevant, improve their skills, and adapt to evolving industry trends. Continuous learning ensures that project managers remain at the forefront of best practices and maintain a competitive edge in the market.

a. Importance of Lifelong Learning: Lifelong learning is a mindset that values continuous improvement. Embracing this approach enables project managers to remain agile, innovative, and adaptable throughout their careers.

b. Options for Continuing Education: Project managers have various options for continuing education, including:

- Professional Development Courses: Specialized courses focused on specific project management methodologies, tools, or industries.

- Workshops and Webinars: Interactive sessions that provide insights into emerging trends and practical applications.

- Certifications: Advanced certifications that validate expertise and knowledge in specialized areas of project management.

- Conferences and Events: Industry conferences that offer networking opportunities and access to industry thought leaders.

- Self-Paced Learning: Online platforms that provide flexible learning opportunities for project managers to study at their own pace.

5.2 The Role of a Mentor:

Having a mentor can be highly beneficial for project managers seeking career development and personal growth. A mentor provides guidance, support, and valuable insights based on their experience, helping mentees navigate challenges and make informed decisions.

a. Benefits of Having a Mentor:

- Personalized Guidance: A mentor offers personalized advice tailored to the mentee's specific needs and goals.

- Expanded Network: Mentors can introduce their mentees to valuable connections within the industry.

- Knowledge Sharing: Mentors share their experiences, successes, and failures, allowing mentees to learn from real-world situations.

- Boosting Confidence: The support and encouragement from a mentor can boost a mentee's confidence in their abilities.

b. Tips for Finding a Suitable Mentor:

- Seek Alignment: Look for a mentor whose expertise, career trajectory, and values align with your own goals and aspirations.

- Be Proactive: Reach out to potential mentors and express your interest in establishing a mentoring relationship.

- Be Open to Feedback: Be receptive to feedback and willing to act upon the advice provided by your mentor.

5.3 Becoming a Mentor:

Becoming a mentor to less experienced project managers is a fulfilling way for experienced professionals to give back to the community and contribute to the growth of the project management field.

a. Benefits of Becoming a Mentor:

- Skill Development: Mentoring enhances leadership, communication, and coaching skills in the mentor.

- Legacy and Impact: Mentors leave a lasting impact on the mentees' careers and contribute to the development of future project management leaders.

- Fresh Perspectives: Mentoring exposes mentors to new ideas and challenges, fostering continued learning and growth.

b. Skills and Qualities of an Effective Mentor:

- Active Listening: Mentors must listen attentively to their mentees' concerns and experiences to provide relevant guidance.

- Empathy and Patience: Being empathetic and patient helps mentors support their mentees through challenges and setbacks.

- Constructive Feedback: Mentors should offer constructive feedback to help mentees improve their skills and decision-making.

- Encouragement: Providing encouragement and motivation boosts mentees' confidence and self-belief.

Conclusion:

Chapter 5 highlights the importance of training, coaching, and mentoring in project management. Continuing education ensures project managers remain current and adaptable in the ever-evolving field. A mentor plays a vital role in providing guidance and support to mentees, facilitating their career development and growth. Additionally, experienced project managers can benefit from becoming mentors, as it helps them enhance their skills and contribute to the future of the profession. By embracing training, coaching, and mentoring, project managers can establish a solid foundation for personal and professional success in the dynamic world of project management.

Chapter 7: Attitude and Leadership in Project Management

"The greatest discovery of all time is that a person can change his future by merely changing his attitude." - Oprah Winfrey.

This chapter focuses on the impact of attitude on success and explores the critical role of leadership in project management.

6.1 Importance of Attitude:

Attitude plays a significant role in project management, influencing the overall success of a project and the effectiveness of a project manager. A positive attitude is particularly vital as it can empower project managers to navigate challenges, inspire their teams, and achieve project goals.

a. Overcoming Challenges: In the face of obstacles and setbacks, a positive attitude allows project managers to maintain resilience and seek solutions rather than succumbing to negativity.

b. Motivating Teams: Project managers with a positive attitude inspire and motivate their teams, creating a collaborative and productive work environment.

c. Achieving Project Goals: A positive attitude drives determination and commitment, leading project managers to stay focused on the project's vision and goals.

Strategies for Maintaining a Positive Attitude:

i. Mindfulness: Practicing mindfulness helps project managers stay present and manage stress effectively.

ii. Gratitude: Cultivating gratitude by acknowledging achievements and positive aspects of the project boosts morale and maintains a positive outlook.

iii. Self-Care: Taking care of one's physical and emotional well-being is crucial for maintaining a positive attitude during challenging times.

6.2 Leadership in Project Management:

Leadership skills are essential for project managers as they are responsible for guiding and inspiring their teams to achieve project objectives successfully. Effective leadership enhances team performance, fosters collaboration, and ensures project success.

a. Different Leadership Styles: There are various leadership styles applicable to project management, including:

- Transformational Leadership: Inspires and motivates teams by setting high expectations and encouraging innovation and creativity.

- Situational Leadership: Adapts leadership style based on the specific needs and maturity level of the team.

- Servant Leadership: Puts the needs of team members first and focuses on supporting and empowering them to excel.

b. Applicability of Leadership Styles:

- Transformational Leadership: Effective in projects that require innovation and creativity, fostering a culture of continuous improvement.

- Situational Leadership: Valuable in dynamic project environments where flexibility in leadership approach is necessary.

- Servant Leadership: Suitable for projects that prioritize team collaboration and inclusivity.

6.3 Developing an Unstoppable Attitude and Leadership Skills:

Cultivating a resilient and proactive attitude, along with developing essential leadership skills, is crucial for project managers to thrive in their roles and drive project success.

a. Resilient Attitude:

- Embrace Change: Viewing change as an opportunity for growth and learning enables project managers to adapt more effectively.

- Learn from Failures: Rather than dwelling on failures, focus on the lessons they offer for improvement and future success.

b. Developing Leadership Skills:

- Effective Communication: Project managers must be skilled communicators to convey expectations, provide feedback, and resolve conflicts.

- Decision-Making: Strong decision-making skills involve assessing risks, gathering information, and choosing the best course of action.

- Problem-Solving: Effective problem-solving requires analytical thinking and creativity to overcome challenges.

Techniques for Developing Leadership Skills:

i. Learning from Leaders: Observe and learn from experienced project managers or leaders in the organization.

ii. Seek Feedback: Solicit feedback from team members and stakeholders to identify areas for improvement.

iii. Professional Development: Participate in leadership development programs, workshops, or courses.

Conclusion:

A positive attitude empowers project managers to overcome challenges, inspire their teams, and achieve project goals. Effective leadership skills enable project managers to guide their teams with confidence, foster collaboration, and drive project success. Cultivating an unstoppable attitude involves practicing mindfulness, gratitude, and self-care. Developing leadership skills requires continuous learning, seeking feedback, and participating in professional development opportunities. By nurturing an unwavering attitude and honing leadership skills, project managers can thrive in their roles, inspire their teams, and lead projects to success.

Chapter 8: The Importance of Technological Knowledge

"The advance of technology is based on making it fit in so that you don't really even notice it, so it's part of everyday life."

- Bill Gates.

This chapter discusses the importance of staying abreast of technological advancements and fostering an innovative mindset in project management.

7.1 Keeping Up with Technology:

In today's fast-paced world, project managers must stay informed about technological advancements relevant to their industries. Technology plays a transformative role in project management practices, and being up-to-date with the latest tools and trends is crucial for project success.

a. Impact on Project Management Practices: Technology has revolutionized project management in various ways, including:

- Communication: Advanced communication tools and platforms facilitate real-time collaboration among team members, stakeholders, and clients.

- Project Tracking: Project management software provides robust tracking and reporting capabilities, enabling project managers to monitor progress effectively.

- Automation: Automation streamlines repetitive tasks, saving time and resources while minimizing errors.

b. Leveraging Technological Advancements: Project managers who embrace technology can improve efficiency, enhance decision-making, and deliver projects more effectively.

7.2 The Role of Innovation:

Driving innovation is vital for project managers as it enables them to find creative solutions to complex challenges and deliver unique and value-added projects.

a. Fostering an Innovative Mindset: Project managers can cultivate an innovative culture by:

- Encouraging Idea Sharing: Creating a safe space for team members to share their ideas and contribute to project innovation.

- Embracing Risk-Taking: Encouraging calculated risk-taking encourages the exploration of new approaches and possibilities.

b. Promoting Creativity: Encouraging creativity through brainstorming sessions and design thinking methodologies sparks innovative ideas and solutions.

c. Embracing Continuous Improvement: An innovative mindset involves embracing continuous improvement and learning from both successes and failures.

7.3 Overcoming a Defeatist Mindset:

A defeatist mindset, especially regarding technology, can hinder a project manager's ability to adapt and leverage the full potential of available tools and advancements.

a. The Dangers of a Defeatist Mindset: A defeatist attitude can lead to:

- Resistance to Change: Fear of new technologies or methodologies can lead to resistance to necessary advancements.
- Missed Opportunities: Refusing to explore new technologies may result in missed opportunities for efficiency gains and improved project outcomes.

b. Strategies for Developing a Growth Mindset:

- Embrace Lifelong Learning: Adopt a mindset of continuous learning and be open to exploring new technologies and approaches.
- Seek Training: Participate in training programs or workshops to build technological skills and knowledge.
- Learn from Failures: View setbacks as learning experiences, and use them to improve future approaches.

c. Emphasize the Benefits: Focus on the potential benefits of embracing new technologies, such as improved productivity, streamlined processes, and enhanced collaboration.

Conclusion:

Understand the significance of technological knowledge in project management. Staying informed about technological advancements empowers project managers to leverage tools and trends that enhance project success. An innovative mindset enables project managers to drive creativity, explore new possibilities, and find unique solutions to challenges. Overcoming a defeatist attitude regarding technology is crucial for embracing growth and seizing opportunities for improvement. By embracing technology, fostering innovation, and cultivating a growth mindset, project managers can thrive in an ever-changing technological landscape and lead projects to greater success.

.

Chapter 9: Stepping Up Your Game

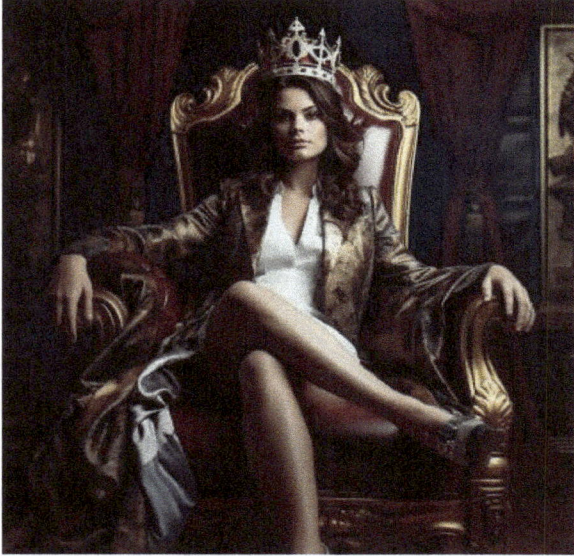

"The only limit to our realization of tomorrow will be our doubts of today." - Franklin D. Roosevelt.

This chapter encourages project managers to deepen their skills, master the craft, and explore different lenses of project management.

8.1 Deepening Your Knowledge:

Mastering advanced project management techniques and tools is essential for project managers seeking to excel in their roles and deliver successful projects. Deepening knowledge in various areas enhances a project manager's ability to tackle complex challenges and make informed decisions.

a. Risk Management: Advanced risk management techniques involve identifying potential risks, analyzing their impacts, and developing effective mitigation strategies to minimize their effects on the project.

b. Quality Management: Mastering quality management ensures that project deliverables meet or exceed the desired standards, resulting in higher customer satisfaction and project success.

c. Schedule Development: Advanced schedule development techniques involve creating realistic and achievable project timelines while considering resource constraints and uncertainties.

8.2 Mastering the Craft:

Truly mastering the craft of project management goes beyond basic knowledge and involves a combination of practical experience, continuous learning, and adaptability.

a. Practical Experience: Hands-on experience in managing projects across various complexities and industries provides invaluable insights and problem-solving skills.

b. Continuous Learning: A commitment to continuous learning allows project managers to stay up-to-date with industry trends, best practices, and emerging technologies.

c. Adaptability: Being adaptable to different project scenarios and environments is vital for responding to changing circumstances and ensuring project success.

8.3 Project Management Lenses:

Understanding different approaches to project management is essential as projects vary in scope, nature, and requirements. Project managers should be adept at selecting and implementing the right approach for each project.

a. Agile: Agile project management focuses on flexibility, collaboration, and iterative development, making it suitable for complex and evolving projects.

b. Hybrid: Hybrid project management combines elements from different methodologies to cater to specific project needs and constraints.

c. Predictive: Predictive project management relies on a well-defined plan and fixed scope, making it suitable for projects with clear requirements and limited changes.

Guidance on Choosing and Implementing the Right Approach:

i. Project Characteristics: Evaluate project characteristics, such as scope, complexity, and uncertainty, to determine the most suitable approach.

ii. Stakeholder Involvement: Consider the level of stakeholder involvement and engagement required in the project.

iii. Project Team Expertise: Assess the project team's expertise and experience with different methodologies to ensure successful implementation.

iv. Project Requirements: Align the chosen approach with the project's specific requirements and deliverables.

Conclusion:

Chapter 8 emphasizes the importance of advanced project management skills in achieving exceptional project outcomes. Deepening knowledge in areas like risk management, quality management, and schedule development empowers project managers to handle project complexities effectively. Mastering the craft involves gaining practical experience, embracing continuous learning, and remaining adaptable in a dynamic environment. Understanding and selecting the right project management approach (agile, hybrid, predictive) ensures projects are delivered successfully, catering to their unique characteristics and requirements. By stepping up their game and honing advanced project management skills, project managers can elevate their performance, lead successful projects, and contribute to organizational growth and success.

Chapter 10: Overcoming Imposter Syndrome and Navigating Office Politics

"Don't doubt yourself, that's what haters are for."

- Turcois Ominek.

This chapter explores the common issue of imposter syndrome among project managers and provides strategies to navigate office politics successfully.

9.1 Understanding Imposter Syndrome:

Imposter syndrome is a psychological pattern where individuals doubt their accomplishments, feel like frauds, and fear being exposed as incompetent, despite evidence of their competence and success. It is prevalent among project managers, especially in high-pressure environments.

a. Impact on Project Managers: Imposter syndrome can undermine a project manager's confidence, decision-making, and ability to lead effectively.

b. Strategies for Overcoming Imposter Syndrome:

- Acknowledge Feelings: Recognize and acknowledge imposter feelings as a normal part of the human experience.

- Focus on Achievements: Reflect on past achievements and successes to reaffirm your competence.

- Seek Support: Share your feelings with trusted colleagues, mentors, or friends who can provide encouragement and perspective.

- Embrace Growth Mindset: Emphasize learning and growth rather than perfection and embrace challenges as opportunities for development.

9.2 Navigating Office Politics:

Office politics refers to the complex dynamics and power struggles that occur in organizational settings. As project managers operate within diverse teams and stakeholder environments, understanding and navigating office politics is crucial.

a. The Role of Office Politics: Office politics can influence decision-making, resource allocation, and project outcomes, impacting project success.

b. Strategies for Navigating Politics Effectively and Ethically:

- Build Relationships: Cultivate positive relationships with colleagues and stakeholders to create a supportive network.

- Stay Neutral: Avoid taking sides in internal conflicts and maintain objectivity in project-related matters.

- Focus on Project Goals: Keep the project's objectives at the forefront and align decisions with the best interests of the project and organization.

- Be Transparent: Practice open communication and transparency to build trust and credibility with team members and stakeholders.

9.3 Speaking Up:

Assertiveness is a crucial skill for project managers to communicate effectively and ensure project success. Being assertive allows project managers to express their thoughts, ideas, and concerns confidently and respectfully.

a. The Importance of Assertiveness: Assertiveness empowers project managers to:

- Advocate for their project and team's needs.

- Address conflicts and resolve issues proactively.

- Clearly communicate expectations and project requirements.

b. Strategies for Effective and Respectful Communication:

- Use "I" Statements: Express thoughts and concerns using "I" statements to avoid sounding accusatory.

- Active Listening: Practice active listening to understand others' perspectives fully before responding.

- Be Solution-Oriented: Offer solutions when raising concerns, rather than simply pointing out problems.

- Manage Emotions: Control emotions during discussions to maintain a professional and constructive atmosphere.

Conclusion:

Chapter 9 goes into essential aspects of project management, addressing imposter syndrome, office politics, and assertiveness. Overcoming imposter syndrome requires acknowledging feelings and emphasizing growth. Navigating office politics demands building positive relationships, staying neutral, and prioritizing project goals. Being assertive enables effective communication, conflict resolution, and advocating for the project and team. By understanding and mastering these elements, project managers can enhance their leadership skills, navigate complex organizational dynamics, and drive successful project outcomes.

Chapter 11: Pursuing Excellence in Project Management

"We are what we repeatedly do. Excellence, then, is not an act,

but a habit." - Aristotle.

This chapter is a call to action for all project managers to strive for excellence and adopt a proactive approach towards their craft.

10.1 Striving for Excellence:

Striving for excellence in all aspects of project management is the hallmark of a successful project manager. Pursuing excellence involves continuously seeking ways to improve performance, deliver exceptional results, and exceed stakeholders' expectations.

a. Importance of Excellence: Excellence in project management leads to:

- High-Quality Deliverables: Projects that meet or exceed quality standards and client expectations.

- Efficient Processes: Streamlined and optimized project management processes that save time and resources.

- Client Satisfaction: Delighting clients by consistently delivering successful projects on time and within budget.

b. Examples of Excellence in Project Management:

- Effective Communication: Clear and timely communication with stakeholders ensures everyone is aligned and informed throughout the project.

- Agile Adaptability: Embracing agile principles enables project managers to respond flexibly to changing requirements and priorities.

- Continuous Improvement: Pursuing continuous improvement and learning from past projects leads to increased efficiency and effectiveness.

10.2 Proactive Project Management:

Taking a proactive approach to project management empowers project managers to anticipate challenges and opportunities, leading to better project outcomes.

a. Benefits of Proactive Project Management:

- Risk Mitigation: Identifying and addressing potential risks early minimizes their impact on the project.

- Efficient Resource Allocation: Proactively managing resources ensures optimal utilization and avoids bottlenecks.

- Stakeholder Alignment: Engaging stakeholders proactively builds trust and facilitates collaboration.

b. Strategies for Proactive Project Management:

- Proactive Planning: Anticipate potential roadblocks and develop contingency plans to handle uncertainties.

- Risk Management: Conduct thorough risk assessments and implement mitigation strategies.

- Stakeholder Engagement: Involve stakeholders from the beginning to ensure alignment and gain their support.

10.3 The Path to Success:

Project managers who strive for excellence open doors to various career paths and opportunities for growth.

a. Potential Career Paths:

- Senior Project Manager: Taking on larger and more complex projects as a senior project manager.

- Program Manager: Overseeing multiple interconnected projects within a program.

- Portfolio Manager: Managing a portfolio of projects aligned with organizational goals.

b. Importance of Continuous Learning and Development:

- Professional Certifications: Obtaining advanced certifications demonstrates expertise and dedication to professional growth.

- Leadership Development: Developing leadership skills enhances the ability to lead larger teams and complex projects.

- Industry Specialization: Pursuing expertise in specific industries opens opportunities for specialized projects and roles.

Conclusion:

Chapter 10 highlights the significance of pursuing excellence in project management. Striving for excellence leads to high-quality deliverables, efficient processes, and satisfied clients. A proactive approach empowers project managers to address challenges, optimize resources, and build strong stakeholder relationships. Achieving excellence opens various career paths, such as senior project manager, program manager, and portfolio manager. Continuous learning and development are vital for advancing in the field and becoming a respected leader in project management. By embracing excellence, proactivity, and continuous growth, project managers can achieve success, drive exceptional projects, and make a significant impact on their organizations.

Chapter 12: Coaching and Mentoring: Next Steps

"The delicate balance of mentoring someone is not creating them in your own image, but giving them the opportunity to create themselves." - Steven Spielberg.

This final chapter discusses the crucial role of coaching and mentoring in ongoing professional development and provides resources for the journey towards becoming an exemplary project manager.

11.1 Continued Development:

Coaching and mentoring play a crucial role in the continued professional development of project managers. They provide valuable guidance, support, and insights that help project managers enhance their skills, overcome challenges, and achieve their career goals.

a. Coaching: Coaching involves a structured and goal-oriented process where a coach helps project managers identify their strengths, weaknesses, and areas for improvement. Coaches provide feedback, encouragement, and accountability to drive growth and development.

b. Mentoring: Mentoring involves a more informal and nurturing relationship where an experienced mentor shares their knowledge, experiences, and wisdom with less experienced project managers. Mentors offer valuable insights and advice based on their own career journey.

11.2 Resources for Development:

To further their development, project managers can explore various resources that offer specialized knowledge, insights, and networking opportunities.

a. Books:

- "The 21 Irrefutable Laws of Leadership" by John C. Maxwell

- "The 360 Degree Leader" by John C. Maxwell

- "The 5 Levels of Leadership" by John C. Maxwell

b. Courses and Workshops:

- Project Management Institute (PMI) Continuing Education Webinars

- Agile Project Management Training

- Leadership Development Workshops

c. Professional Organizations:

- Project Management Institute (PMI)

- Agile Alliance

d. Webinars and Podcasts:

- Project Leadership Institute Podcast

- The PMP Exam Radioshow

11.3 Next Steps:

Project managers seeking to elevate their skills to the next level can take specific steps to set clear career goals and create a comprehensive development plan.

a. Setting Career Goals:

- Identify Aspirations: Define the long-term goals you want to achieve in your project management career.

- Set SMART Goals: Create specific, measurable, achievable, relevant, and time-bound goals that align with your aspirations.

b. Creating a Development Plan:

- Self-Assessment: Conduct a self-assessment to identify areas of strengths and areas that need improvement.

- Seek Feedback: Obtain feedback from colleagues, mentors, or supervisors to gain insights into your performance and growth opportunities.

- Choose Developmental Activities: Select courses, workshops, or coaching sessions that align with your career goals and development needs.

- Networking: Engage in networking opportunities to build connections and stay updated on industry trends and best practices.

c. Implementing the Plan:

- Take Action: Actively participate in the chosen developmental activities and implement the knowledge gained into your projects.

- Track Progress: Monitor your progress regularly and make adjustments as needed to stay on track.

Conclusion:

Chapter 11 emphasizes the importance of coaching and mentoring in project managers' continued development. Leveraging coaching and mentoring relationships empowers project managers to receive personalized guidance and insights to enhance their skills and career trajectory. Various resources, such as books, courses, professional organizations, webinars, and podcasts, are available for further development. To take their skills to the next level, project managers should set clear career goals, create a development plan, and actively implement their learning. By investing in continued development and taking strategic steps towards their career goals, project managers can achieve excellence in their profession and make a lasting impact in the field of project management.

Chapter 13: PDUs

"Education is the most powerful weapon which you can use to

change the world." - Nelson Mandela

Professional Development Units (PDUs) are not merely a requisite but a beacon for continuous growth in the realm of project management. Every three years, the Project Management Institute mandates PMP certificate holders to acquire 60 PDUs. However, the essence of these units extends far beyond a mere number.

Instead of passively accumulating PDUs through any available video or webinar, I urge you to approach this with intention and strategy. Envision each PDU as an opportunity to elevate your prowess in project management. Whether it's mastering the intricacies of scheduling, venturing deeper into agile practices, or enhancing your skills in stakeholder management, each learning avenue should be pursued with earnestness and purpose.

It's easy to be swayed by the allure of 'free' or 'cheap' PDUs, but I implore you to shift your focus. Ask yourself: "What value does this bring to my professional journey?" Time, as they say, is the most precious currency. A webinar might not have a price tag, but if it doesn't enrich your knowledge or skills, is it truly worth your time?

Instead of merely seeking cost-effectiveness, prioritize the value proposition. Sometimes, an investment might seem substantial upfront, but the returns – in terms of knowledge, expertise, and growth – can be invaluable.

Moreover, the avenues to earn PDUs are diverse. From practicing project management, presenting webinars, attending training sessions, to mentoring and being mentored – each path offers a unique learning experience. Embrace these opportunities not as mere obligations but as steppingstones to your professional zenith.

As your mentor and guide, I encourage you to approach your PDU journey with discernment and passion. Remember, it's not about ticking off a checklist; it's about enriching your craft and, in turn, the world of project management.

About the Author

Phill C. Akinwale, PMP has managed operational endeavors, projects and project controls across government and private sectors in various companies, including Motorola, Honeywell, Emerson, Skillsoft, Citigroup, Iron Mountain, Brown and Caldwell, US Airways and CVS Caremark. With his extensive experience in various facets of Project Management and rigorous project controls, he has trained project management worldwide (NASA, FBI, USAF, USACE, US Army, Department of Transport) across five PMBOK® Guide editions over the last 15 years.

He holds twelve project management certifications with six in Agile Project Management (CSM, PMI-ACP, PSM, PSPO, PAL, SPS). As a John Maxwell Certified Coach and Speaker, Phill delivers workshops, seminars, keynote speaking, and coaching in leadership and soft skills. Working together with you and your team or organization, he will guide you in the desired direction and equip you to reach your goals. Books he has authored include: The No-Good Leader, Earned Value Basics and Project Management Mid-Level to C-Level.

www.ingramcontent.com/pod-product-compliance
Lightning Source LLC
Chambersburg PA
CBHW071119210326
41519CB00020B/6348